THE POWER OF ONE

The Power of One

The Story of Elaine Bannon and the People of Rombo, Kenya

KATHLEEN O'KEEFFE

VERITAS

Published 2008 by
Veritas Publications
7/8 Lower Abbey Street
Dublin 1, Ireland

Email publications@veritas.ie
Website www.veritas.ie

ISBN 978-1-84730-126-0

10 9 8 7 6 5 4 3 2 1

Designed by Lir Mac Cárthaigh
Printed in Ireland by ColourBooks Ltd, Dublin

Veritas books are printed on paper made from the wood pulp of managed forests. For every tree felled, at least one tree is planted, thereby renewing natural resources.

Contents

Foreword

ONE BY ONE the Maasai women spat on Elaine. She had given up her comfortable house and good lifestyle in Ireland, said goodbye to her family and friends, and embarked on a journey of working with and for the Maasai. This was not the welcome she had expected. What she didn't know then was that spitting in the Maasai world is a form of blessing.

In Africa, more people die of hunger than AIDS, polio, malaria and TB combined. Elaine Bannon knew these facts. She knew that a child dies every seventeen seconds from drinking dirty water; she did not know that this would one day happen while she held a child in her arms. Elaine, nevertheless, was determined rather than disheartened when confronted by these statistics.

I have known Elaine for twenty-five years and I have watched her evolve and take her place in the 'real' world. I visit Elaine every year and see the real and sustainable difference she is making in the lives of thousands of children. I am a friend and supporter. Now in my late forties, I have joined the thousands of people around the world that have decided to 'give something back'. Most people struggle to find a way to do this. I found Elaine Bannon.

The bush is alive with jungle sounds. On her first day in Rombo, Kenya, she asks a tall Maasai warrior where the toilet is located. He points to the bush. Elaine is scared, but needs must. She is aware there are dangerous snakes, elephants and hyenas everywhere, but still she wanders deep into the bush to get a comfortable distance from the gathering. As she squats she feels something crawling up her leg. She screams and runs back to the group. They laugh at the *musungo* (white person) and go about their business of killing a goat to celebrate Elaine's arrival. Five years later, Elaine is more at home in the bush than on Grafton Street.

Elaine has brought me (and the author of this book) on a fascinating journey. She has made me challenge myself physically and mentally. The physical hardship of life in the bush can be managed, but the mental journey to understand why things are the way they are in the world today is very tough. Essential reading, such as books by Jeffrey Sachs, have helped, but ultimately you must stand in the red dusty earth of Africa and work it out for yourself.

This is a tough journey indeed, but a hugely rewarding one. My work on the ground and my studies have made me a more complete person and I am aware that I am gaining as much as I am giving in this equation. You quickly realise that Africa's problems are not all about corruption and laziness; in fact, they are about poor infrastructure and communications, climate, geography, disease, trade and so on.

During Elaine's journey we have come across extraordinary people. Some people open doors and some close them. One quickly learns not to take no for an answer, especially when you are aware that children's lives are at stake due to indifference. I have watched Elaine get angry with a Maasai chief until he finally negotiated and gave her what she needed, and I have watched her cry while listening to the plight of a young girl facing genital mutilation.

The involvement of Irish people and other people from around the world helps to value Elaine's work. She rarely feels isolated when she can call home for help. Elaine continues to do wonderful things and she has realised that education is the way to freedom for Africa's people. Every day she encounters the fruits of her labour, and every day she laughs and cries with her Maasai friends. They face challenges together and they have achieved a huge amount.

Gandhi said, 'You must be the change you want to see in the world', and Elaine Bannon is living that to the full.

MATT PORTER, October 2008

— Introduction —
The Power of One

ON THE EAST COAST of Africa, the former British colony, Kenya, faces the Indian Ocean. By contrast with its neighbours, Ethiopia and Tanzania, it is small, but when one is used to travelling manageable distances on good roads, it seems vast and, at times, frightening. From Mombasa, with its wonderful palm beaches, to the fertile highlands on the slopes of Mount Kenya, and on to the barren Turkana desert, the terrain is constantly changing.

The variety of wildlife, which is the main tourist attraction, gives an exotic feeling to the landscape, especially at dawn and at sunset. Tourism has become a very important industry in Kenya because of this, and the charm and warmth of the people makes the visitor feel welcome. Films such as *Out of Africa* have been instrumental in letting the world know about Kenya's majesty and mystery, and in recent years a very efficient air service to the capital, Nairobi, and to Mombasa has made the tropical country a place where Americans and Europeans spend their holidays.

Unfortunately, Kenya's economy is dependent on tourism and a few cash crops – tea, coffee and fruit. Today, with the threat of global warming, all these are vulnerable, with both the irrigation for the crops and the habitats of the animals beginning to feel the strain. Kenya has none of the high-earning minerals of South Africa, nor the oilfields of West Africa.

The scourge of AIDS has caused huge suffering in the past twenty years, and in places such as Mombasa the orphans left by the terrible epidemic roam the streets in search of food and shelter. They are prey to all kinds of exploitation, and in a country where education is for the lucky rather than for all its citizens, their hopes for the future are pretty grim.

The Kenyan people are varied in their features and their tribal attributes. The Kikuyu are the 'Kerrymen' of Kenya (a name given to them by the Irish missionaries). They live in the Rift Valley and are hard working and intelligent. It was they who spilled their blood for independence. The first president of Kenya – Jomo Kenyatta – was a Kikuyu. When the white settlers left in the 1960s the Kikuyu were the ones who had the money and the know-how to cultivate the land, and their children had the best education, which led to the best jobs in the capital. They are envied, and often even hated by the other tribes. Physically they are tall and strong. The Kamba tribe is very different. They are small in stature, pleasant and easy-going, but because they live around Machokos, where it is dry and hot, experience has taught them that planting crops is futile.

Among the many other tribes who live in rural areas and along the coast are the Maasai. For long before recorded history, the Maasai tribe has survived by following the herds of cattle from one pasture ground to another according to where grass becomes available in the rainy seasons. However, with the encroachment of the desert (at the rate of more than thirty kilometres a year) their way of life is seriously threatened. The Maasai are tall and elegantly built. They consider themselves the owners of all the land and cattle on earth – an attitude that had them in constant conflict with the white settlers of colonial times. They had no compunction about pasturing their animals on the fertile ranches of the white men, stealing their cattle in night raids, and leaving a trail of disease – picked up from the wild animals they had encountered on their journeys.

Maasailand in southern Kenya is a man's world. Girls are just a commodity and are sold into marriage for a cow, two goats or, in cold weather, a blanket. Prior to marriage they are circumcised. A more accurate term for this would be female genital mutilation, considered a rite of passage into womanhood. After this procedure many women bleed to death; others become infected due to the use of dirty knives or blades; and all suffer enormously when giving birth.

There is a Chinese saying: 'May you live in interesting times', and the Maasai men would feel the full effect of this in a world that is changing their status vis-à-vis their women at a very rapid pace. The women are to the forefront in their desire for education and a safer, better life, and the identity of the men as warriors is being threatened. Their way of life is being eroded with global warming and they are being forced to seek an alternative way or die.

Into this world came Elaine Bannon, a Dublin woman taking a holiday from her high-powered managerial job. She saw the needs of the people and in particular the plight of the women, and felt she had to do something about it. So in 2002, she gave up her job, sold her fairly plush car and threw in her lot with people about whom she knew very little.

Elaine was born in Dublin in 1962, the first child of Maureen Lane and Dan Bannon. She grew up in Elm Mount Avenue, in Beaumont, when it was a relatively new estate, with crowds of children her own age. Her father, Dan, spent his Saturdays in the local park, organising games for these children. Her mother was well known for being the 'mammy' who would join anyone – from zero to ninety – in their sorrows. From the beginning, Elaine was accustomed to having a constant parade of visitors, many of them very needy, in her home. There was a general acceptance that times like Christmas were more for giving than for receiving, and Maureen had 'clients' for whom she was ready to make inroads into all family coffers when the need arose! On Dan's side of the family there was a missionary priest, a missionary sister and a lay missionary. At school in the 1960s it was commonplace to have regular collections for the 'black babies'. Fund-raising was in the air, but if you were a Bannon it was in your blood as well! As time went by, Elaine read about the work of 'Mama Tina' Noble in

Vietnam and Papa Jamie with the sewer children of South America. She helped the usual charitable organisations and was an active member of Amnesty International. Her education had been that of the average Irish girl of her time: attending the local primary school – Holy Child, Larkhill, which was run by the Holy Faith Sisters; then attending Margaret Alwyard secondary school; and eventually studying at Whitehall House, where she did a secretarial course. Having finished this she worked in various offices, always advancing to higher levels of responsibility, until at the start of the year 2000 she held a well-paying managerial post. As the new millennium dawned, Elaine's life seemed destined to be the ordinary life of any Irish career woman of her era, but fate and faith produced another scenario – and she was ready for the challenge.

In 2002 Elaine went on a holiday to Kenya, and was shocked by the poverty she saw all around her. As she reflected on this she felt that she had to do something about it. She had made contacts in Mombasa, so when she decided to return to Kenya and give some assistance, she connected with the Kenyan she had met while on holiday and for a year she worked to help AIDS orphans in the district of Mombasa. By the end of the year she had made other contacts, and they explained to her that though things were bad in the city, at least there were some services, but in country areas, for example Rombo in southern Kenya, people were hungry and in great need of help, especially to get clean water, education and health care. Elaine was prevailed upon to go and see for herself, and what she saw convinced her that her real call was to the Rombo area and its 30,000 people. To most of us, a single woman with no organisation behind her setting out to help people who were destitute might seem totally ludicrous, but Elaine had faith, conviction and a huge heart, and to her that was reason enough to tackle such a job.

When Elaine decided to go to Kenya it took a while for family and friends to take her actions seriously, but when they did they came fully on board and were generous in financing her projects. Help often came from unlikely sources, and many contacts from her life in the busy world of industry mounted fund-raising campaigns on her behalf and helped her financially. An engineer, Matt Porter, who was a member of Rotary Ireland, used his not inconsiderable energy and charm to get donations from members on both sides of the border, and made valuable contacts for her with members of the Rotary clubs abroad. Danny Slevin, a work associate and musician, held gigs and made CDs to raise funds. The road on which Elaine grew up, Elm Mount Avenue, Beaumont, went into action with a vengeance, with people holding coffee mornings and cheese and wine tastings, and children hosting 'Bring and Buy' sales. With her managerial skills, Elaine focused on the biggest needs – clean water, education and health care. The field of endeavour was vast, but warm and generous hearts had been touched. A fire had been ignited and it began to give light and warmth.

— I —

A Global Issue

HUMAN ACTIVITY ASSOCIATED with burning fossil fuel has resulted in a change in the chemistry of the atmosphere. As the volume of greenhouse gas increases, the temperature of the earth's atmosphere rises gradually. Statistics show that nine of the ten hottest years since records began have occurred since 1983. Desertification, already happening in sub-tropical regions, will continue apace. The melting of the ice sheets at the Arctic and Antarctic is manifest in the rise of sea levels, the depletion in marine life and the greater frequency and intensity of hurricanes. Scientists foretell that huge shifts will occur in rainfall patterns. The poor in the northern half of Africa face extinction unless we in the less threatened areas, who are mostly to blame for the rapid changes in climate, reconsider our actions.

In the West we have grown accustomed to a self-indulgent lifestyle. The older people among us will remember clearly the days when all the water for domestic use had to be brought from the nearest well. When one knew the feel of heavy buckets, one was unlikely to waste a drop. Turf was the main source of energy for cooking and heating the home, and after the hot summers of back-breaking work in the bog the supply of turf was treated with care. Food was simple, and families in rural areas were self-sufficient. It was in similar circumstances that Elaine found herself with the Maasai people.

When Elaine first went to Kenya she worked near Mombasa. Within a year she realised that parts of southern Kenya were far more needy, and possibilities for giving new hope were beckoning her. In Rombo, near the Tanzanian border, at the southern end of the Rift Valley and close to two large game parks, Amboseli and Tsavo West, Elaine felt that there must be streams of water close to the surface because of the proximity of Kilimanjaro with its snow-covered peaks. Previously, in spite of this, the Maasai people were often forced to drink cows' urine to prevent dehydration. Here, a population of approximately thirty thousand (the Maasai are nomadic, so exact figures are hard to come by) were living in frightening poverty, and often dying of diseases that could easily be avoided with an adequate supply of clean water and basic instruction on how children and their mothers could be protected from infection.

The mass media are constantly reminding us that we can make a difference, and the will to do this is a new Christian imperative. Jesus tells us repeatedly, 'Love one another', and in 1 John 4:16 we are reminded in uncompromising language: 'He who lives in love lives in God, and God lives in him.'

The kind of Christianity demanded of us today is very different from that with which many of us grew up. We have a duty to know about the problems in our world, and to address them. When documentaries on TV tell us unpalatable truths, we cannot simply switch to another channel and pretend we don't know! We have a duty to look at the unjust social, economic and political structures in our world, and do our part in liberating the imaginations of individuals and Christian communities to find new ways of living that will be just, non-polluting and sustainable. In the Old Testament, the Book of Micah tells that we must 'act justly, love tenderly and walk humbly with our God' (Micah 6:8). It is over two millennia since these words were uttered, but the recipe for happiness does not change! A story of hope from the rich mythology of the East comes to mind when we consider the terrible inequalities of our world:

> A guru asked his disciples the question: 'How do you know when the dawn has come?' Some answered, 'When the light comes through the branches of the trees'. Others thought it was when you saw a figure in the distance and you could differentiate between an animal and a human being. The guru replied: 'No! It is when you look at all people and see that they are your sisters and brothers. Then the dawn has come.'

— 2 —

Water: The Gold of Tomorrow

SCIENTISTS WARN US that the wars of the future will be fought over supplies of clean water. Even today in Ireland we find that every so often a community is warned that the water is polluted and that all water for domestic use will have to be boiled. In the early months of 2007, for example, the citizens of Galway suffered anxiety and hardship because of the threat of water-borne diseases. This had serious effects on the lives of children and the elderly, and caused major problems for those whose earnings from the summer tourist trade were expected to carry them through the rest of the year. The media coverage and the political fallout brought home to us that a lack of clean water can cause a crisis even in a society where bottled water is freely available.

As a result of desertification, Rombo, like all sub-Saharan Africa, is suffering from lack of water – clean or otherwise. The following story will illustrate this.

The local school in Rombo, which had no water supply, asked that all pupils bring one litre of water to school each morning. This water was used to make tea for the teachers and cook food for both staff and pupils. After using this method of getting enough water for domestic use for some months, the deputy headmaster noticed a yellow liquid in some containers. When he asked a senior boy about this he was told, 'Many of us have no means of getting water, so we bring the first urine of the cow every morning'! Elaine recounts a similar story:

> I went to an area where we planned to put a well. The local people offered us tea on arrival. I am not normally a tea drinker but it is an insult to refuse tea in a village. Later in a conversation with the mammas, I asked where they normally got water. They said that the nearest water supply is about eight kilometres away. They make the trek every day with twenty-litre drums, which they carry on their heads. In the dry season there is no water in the stream. It was the dry season, so I asked how they made the tea. They informed me that it was made from milk, and that the utensils were washed in cows' urine! I struggled to keep down the contents of my stomach as the full implications of what I had heard dawned on me. The good news is that I lived to tell the tale!

In Rombo, the water used by most people is from a local stream. The cows and goats get their water supply from the same source, and clothes and bodies are washed there too. The hope is that eventually every person will have access to a proper water source, but despite the fact that in the recent past thirteen wells have been sunk and a seven and a half kilometre pipeline has been laid, bringing clean water to over 3,000 people, the full realisation of this dream is as yet far in the distance.

In Rombo, located at the foot of Kilimanjaro, the melt water from the snow-capped mountain gives hope and the possibility of irrigation. The women, who are the main agriculturalists, are aware of the need for fruit and vegetables to make up a healthy diet. Traditionally, the Maasai survived on milk and meat from the cattle, but the women are open to change and ready to make full use of every opportunity to provide a better future for their families. Irrigation is a key factor in this, and the women are more than willing to dig trenches for pipelines, provided by donations from generous donors. Now, things like tomatoes are a fairly usual produce in the Friday market in Rombo, and the total dependence on cattle-related food is coming to an end. Sunflowers grow easily in the warm climate, and sunflower oil can be sold in the market. The hope is that this new direction in agriculture, as well as providing a balanced diet, will lead to a new source of income, and valuable shillings (Kenya's currency) for school fees. And who knows, perhaps the exclusive safari lodges located in the area will have local suppliers in the future!

The availability of water has huge implications for the future of the Maasai people, and organisations such as the Rotary Club, the Lions club and the Dublin-based Kedington Group are transforming the Rombo area by their generous funding of irrigation schemes. One woman's dream is providing for many!

− 3 −

That they may have
Life to the Full

THE UNITED NATIONS' figures on child survival show progress, which proves that we can do something about the terrible scourge of infant mortality, but when we read a little further in the UNICEF report of 13 September 2007, we find that every year more than twice the population of Ireland is lost in infancy on a worldwide scale! The highest rates of child mortality are found in Africa. The executive director of UNICEF Ireland, Melanie Verwoerd, says the new figures show that progress is possible, if we act with renewed urgency to scale up interventions that have proven successful. There is a clear need for action on child survival in Africa and beyond. In the West, if a child is abducted, savaged by dogs or even killed in an accident, the media is busy asking a myriad of questions, but the fact that a child dies of hunger or disease every second in Africa does not seem to exercise them at all.

We in Ireland are very concerned about health care, and rightly so! Life is God's greatest gift to us and we have a responsibility to protect that gift. There is scarcely a day but some deficiency in our health services is highlighted, and public outrage is visited on the Minister for Health or the health service in general. Anything that might be considered a health hazard is dealt with: for example, the presence of asbestos roofing will have an entire building condemned. We in the First World consider it essential to have health insurance if at all possible. We live in a society that values longevity and is willing to go to great lengths not just to preserve life, but to enhance it, regardless of expense – the rise in popularity of cosmetic surgery bears this out. The average life expectancy of men in Ireland is seventy-five; for women it is even higher, at eighty. In Kenya it is only forty-nine – an age at which we would consider someone to be in the prime of life! From difficult birth to early death, the struggle with disease and malnutrition in Africa is unrelenting.

In the parish of Rombo there is one health centre, which is without a doctor. In Kenya there is 0.1 doctors for every 1,000 people, while in Ireland we have 3 per 1,000. When a woman goes into labour she is helped by a local woman. If the latter is unable to cope, then the expectant mother has to be brought by bicycle (the only form of transport available) to the health centre. This can often be a journey of up to eighty kilometres. If the nurse at the centre is unable to deliver the baby, then a further journey to the nearest hospital ensues. Too often both the mother and the baby die before reaching the hospital.

Elaine's dream is that each of the twenty-one outstations in Rombo would have its own properly staffed and equipped health centre, and that at least one doctor for a cluster of centres would be available.

Over the past twenty years, the AIDS epidemic has increased the need for proper health centres, which would have the capability of screening for the virus. At present, apart from the screening facility in the one health centre in Rombo, there is no way of finding out if somebody is suffering from AIDS, and people in remote villages are buried the day they die because of the temperature, thus diagnosis from post-mortem is impossible. Often people die of tuberculosis, but the suspicion is that the presenting illness is merely the last straw after the virus has eroded the natural immunity of the body. If the disease had been detected in time, perhaps retro viral drugs could have been administered and the person's life spared, as well as the lives of many others who might have been infected by the disease.

Apart from all the physical suffering caused by AIDS, the ramifications for society are enormous. The number of orphans is constantly on the increase, and though the extended family tries to look after the children, they are hugely at risk — too many mouths to feed and too few resources.

More and more women are becoming conscious of the importance of hygiene and its role in the health of their families. They form inspection groups to check latrines and to provide for better ventilation, and, where possible, isolation for tuberculosis sufferers.

While we in the West demand extraordinary means for extending life, the people of Rombo would be happy to have basic health care within reasonable distance of their homes.

— 4 —
St Joseph's House of Hope

EARLY IN THE New Testament we meet Joseph. He was a just man, sensitive to the woman he loved, though utterly confused at what was happening in their lives. He was a man of dreams and, through thick and thin, he followed his dreams. Over the centuries many have turned to him in their need, and people like the great Spanish mystic Teresa of Avila dedicated her many Carmelite convents to him. She looked to him as 'the man who paid the bills'. In his book *Like the River Flowing*, Paulo Coelho tells us that his mother had dedicated him to St Joseph after his very difficult birth and that the saint became the cornerstone of his life. He reminds us that Joseph was constantly being persuaded by an angel to do exactly the opposite to what he intended. He was called to go against what common sense would dictate and he followed the dream that was to play such an important part in our salvation.

Early in 2007, Karen Coleman, radio presenter with Newstalk 106, visited Rombo. After conducting a radio interview with Elaine she wrote an article for the *Sunday Tribune* entitled, 'How Elaine Bannon's Kenyan holiday changed her life'. That article appeared on 30 April, the same day on which the *Sunday Times* listed Ireland's millionaires. Inspired by the huge differences between the two worlds being portrayed, and also by the fact that Elaine's project was entitled 'Joseph House of Hope', a sister of Mercy with a lifetime's experience of St Joseph's gift for fund-raising decided to spend some time the next day (the feast of St Joseph the Worker) writing to those who had an abundance of this world's goods on behalf of those who were in great need. Thus began a campaign to raise funds for the three major needs already mentioned – clean water, education and basic health care in Rombo. At the time of writing this book St Joseph has moved many hearts and loosened the strings of many purses.

It is sometimes forgotten that Knock was the only place that St Joseph ever appeared. There were particular needs in Rombo requiring attention at the time of the anniversary of the apparition at Knock (21 August 2007). That day an email arrived from Kenya saying that a crippled girl who was a gifted tailor had been offered further training in Sweden, but she would have to provide her own passage money. Since this would amount to €800 it seemed impossible. However, a church gate collection was due in Marino parish the following weekend, so the green light was given. (In fact that collection topped €11,000!) Later that day, a young woman who had promised to sponsor a child's education when a church gate collection had been taken at Sunday Mass in Elaine's own parish, Beaumont, came forward to say that she would prefer to give a lump sum rather than commit herself to future payments, which circumstances might make difficult to meet. With extraordinary generosity she offered €800, and handed in the cheque the following morning. The Man of Dreams had made a dream come true for one young Maasai woman, who would in time help others realise their dreams and find a way of living that would enable them and their families to live with dignity.

Lest anybody think that Elaine's native parish had been outdone by a neighbouring parish, it too realised €11,000, not to mention all that the neighbours have given over the years. St Joseph is an excellent provider, especially for those who have big dreams!

For many older people the sense of hopelessness about the faith future of Ireland is a huge cause of sadness. However, experience shows that while some are reluctant to 'practice', there is a strong altruistic spirit. Organisations such as Concern, Goal and Trócaire have been able to continue their massive aid programmes for almost half a century without taking from the hundreds of local charities. St John of the Cross tells us that 'in the evening of life we will be judged on love'. As I have worked to raise funds for Elaine's project in Rombo I have been greatly encouraged, humbled and excited by the sheer generosity of people of all ages.

One morning on my way home from Mass, a friend, a retired woman with no spare cash, handed me an envelope. It was money she had put aside for a winter coat but decided that she could manage without it, and that money went to sponsor a young girl in her final year at a secretarial school. Another woman, who is no longer young and works in the kitchen at the local hospital, apologised that because her heating system had broken down she could only make a small contribution, and this came by post. A mother of four who has more than enough to do to cope with rearing her family tapped into the generosity of a local group and sent €1,000. Chance meetings with people who were strangers led to donations big and small, and many wealthy people gave generously as a result of a letter.

The spirit of neighbourliness, which was always part of the Irish psyche, is very much alive. Yes, we live in a consumer society, and at times we are blown away by the tide of wealth that leads to competitiveness and greed, but deep down we have a desire to go beyond the present with its fears and tensions, and to work for something greater than ourselves. Go into any bookshop and you will find a section on the life of the Spirit. The books may not speak to your traditional beliefs, but they do argue that there is an invisible world where a whole other life is crying out to be lived. Though the official Churches are not as supported as they were in the past, most people will be grateful to be told that prayers are being said for them. When we pray we are meeting our brothers and sisters at a level that is ineffable, and which ever so slightly brings about a little more unity. Some of the most influential psychologists have told us that by *doing* we change our thinking. There are times when we are all reluctant to go the extra mile, but when we do, aren't we glad?

Elaine Bannon – one Irish woman among 30,000 Maasai.

Maasai men and women in traditional and ceremonial dress.

The Maasai women – providing and caring for family.

Basic classroom, but eager to learn.

Making the most of a water tap.

Maasai mother and daughter.

Mother and child in ceremonial dress.

Elaine among friends.

— 5 —
Myths, Facts and 'World' Hunger

OVER THE YEARS I have often been in conversation with well-heeled, sophisticated people who justify their unwillingness to help people in the Third World by trotting out some myths. In response, I have often become so emotional that I have damaged my own cause and left their opinions totally unchanged. However, there are people who are honest questioners and who, when given the facts, are willing to be convinced that we do live in a very unequal world and that we all have a duty to change it, even if only a little.

One of the myths is that money to Third World countries is money down the drain, because there is so little to show for it. The fact is that so little is given, there could not possibly be much to show! The wealthy countries give approximately $30 per African per year. When the money for debt relief, consultants, food and emergency aid is deducted, what we give is $12 per head. Another myth is that all aid programmes fail. If something is not funded properly it cannot succeed. Kenya is a classic example. It needs $1.5 billion, but we give it only $100 million. Better co-ordination amongst governments, aid agencies and the local people would make a huge difference. An intelligent use of resources would give aid programmes the legs to go the whole journey!

Emerging nations need help with their judicial systems and public administration, proper computer systems, accounts, job training and adequate remuneration for work so that people are not in positions where they need bribes to survive. Education is hard to come by in these countries, and to expect the civil services to run smoothly when there has not been any foundation is unrealistic.

We often pontificate on democracy and proclaim that there is no democracy in Africa. In fact, eleven countries are free, twenty are partly free and working on it, and sixteen still suffer under dictatorships. That means that 66 per cent are moving in the right direction. This is an enormous achievement when one considers the long years of foreign colonisation and the various tribal systems that have been the norm since before recorded history.

Another myth is that Africans are lazy. If you can imagine year after year planting crops and waiting for rain that never came or seeing the termites make short work of the crops that seemed to be thriving; or, as is the case frequently with perishable goods like fruit and vegetables, having a good crop but the vehicle you hired to bring it to the market getting stuck in a river swollen by flooding so that the entire harvest is ruined, and yet still having to find money to pay for the transport, would it be easy to find the energy to start again? African farmers are not lazy. They lack machinery, roads, soil nutrients, irrigation, storage facilities, fair trade opportunities, education and knowledge about crop rotation, all of which is readily available to their western counterparts.

When Irish people who have visited Kenya talk about the Maasai tribe, they are often very admiring of the women and very critical of the men. They point out that the women do most of the work and that, apart from looking after their herds, the men seem to make little or no contribution to the upkeep of the family. However, when we look back at the history of Ireland as portrayed in our literature, we find people like James Joyce, J.M. Synge and Sean O'Casey portraying women as strong and determined, thereby emasculating their men. Long after we have been freed from the domination of the colonist, our men seem, at times, to suffer from the legacy of being deprived of the power to work out their destiny for themselves. This, according to the writers, has contributed to a loss of identity, and at times the scourge of alcoholism, which has given us a bad name around the world. We find that a lack of a sense of identity has led to an impression of laziness, but that often it comes from a lack of self-worth.

Kenya too is a country left with the scars of colonialism. The tribal custom of treating the men as warriors was acceptable when they were totally nomadic and had to protect the women and children from wild animals and enemy tribes. However, the increase in global warming has changed their role. The Maasai are now becoming settled. While the men go with their herd from one pasture ground to another, when a rainy season has provided pasture, the women stay at home in the mud huts and the children go to school when at all possible.

The American psychologist William Glasser, who devised a system of educational psychology called Reality Therapy, says that every human being has four basic needs – love and belonging, power, freedom and fun. He holds that if one of these is missing, then the person tries to compensate for this in ways that are damaging to himself or herself and society. If we apply this to the Maasai men, then perhaps the loss of power, which in the past came from being the protector of the tribe, is being compensated for by a drinking culture and *laissez faire* attitude. A Maasai man will buy medicine for a sick cow, but not for a sick child. His entire identity is bound up with ownership of a herd of cattle, so when something like drought or Rift Valley Fever decimates his herd, his outlook is very bleak indeed. This *laissez faire* attitude of Maasai men is changing very slowly. However, those who have been educated (and that number is increasing) are gaining self-respect from real achievements and are becoming genuine leaders.

Perhaps the worst cop-out of all is that we should not do anything by way of aiding the African countries because we are only saving children to become hungry adults. Ironically, the investment in ending extreme poverty will also end the high birth rates in poor countries. As urban life takes off, fewer children will be needed for agriculture and collecting water and wood. As education improves, families will need more money per child and will have fewer children as a result. With education and proper family planning, fewer children will be born. Better health care will decrease the numbers of children dying in infancy and in their early childhood, and having more children to compensate will not be necessary.

Another myth is the idea that there is 'world hunger'. Thankfully, there is not a situation where there is hunger on a world scale – but the fact that we can use the term so easily shows that we have no concept of what it would mean if it were a reality. So why talk about 'world hunger'? It would be far more honest to look at the huge inequalities between First World and Third World and see the reality – need and greed.

The first human right is the right to life. Life has to be sustained by nourishing food, and when a people or nation is deprived of this, then they are, virtually, deprived of an inalienable right. Night after night on our TV screens we see advertisements, documentaries and news items showing children with gaunt faces, bulging eyes and bloated stomachs being held by their grief-stricken mothers who have to watch them slowly die of malnourishment and dehydration. In a world where we are faced with an over-abundance of food, a child dies every second!

Recently, a task force was set up in Ireland under the chairmanship of Professor Jeffrey Sachs, director of the Earth Institute at Columbia University in the US. This task force was called for in last year's white paper on Irish aid. It brings together Irish and international expertise to identify how we can best contribute to tackling the causes of food insecurity, especially in Africa. Dr Josette Sheeran, director of the World Food Programme (WFP), is a member of the task force. In an interview with RTÉ she pointed out that we have reached a critical point because of the rise of commodity prices. The WFP has seen the cost of food increase by over 50 per cent in the past five years, while grain markets are tighter than at any time in recent history. The omens are not good. The dry areas are becoming drier and the wet areas wetter. Dr Sheeran reported that 820 million people are undernourished and 27 per cent of all children under five years old in the developing world are malnourished. Although there has been a small reduction in the proportion of hungry people in the past fifteen years, population growth means that in absolute terms the numbers have increased.

Though the Irish are far from the Maasai in terms of geography, customs and mores, we realise that their social condition is very much like ours was a century ago. Our ancestors had open fires, thatched roofs, families depending on a bread-winner who, with pony and cart, carried goods from one place to another. Our people struggled to give us the opportunities we enjoy today. Hopefully, the seeds of a better future for Kenya are already being planted by people like Elaine Bannon and her warriors.

– 6 –

Women and Powerlessness

IN HER BOOK, *Job's Daughters*, Joan Chittister OSB looks at the status of women in society, with particular emphasis on how, even today, women are often infantilised. She analyses different forms of power and shows how it is almost universally used against women. She points out that exploitative power, which uses another for personal gain, sees the person being exploited as a mere resource for personal advantage. Throughout history women have been sidelined or forgotten about entirely. Studies of slavery ignored them – they were born to be slaves! Amazingly, even enlightened people such as Thomas Aquinas, Plato and Aristotle all saw them as inferior. Many religions have enshrined this inferior status in the marriage service, where the woman is given away by one man into the care of another, and is told to love, honour and obey her husband. Her role was seen as that of housekeeper and child bearer. So 'normal' was this degradation that even those who were being oppressed by it did not notice!

The long history of colonialism in Africa has not only damaged international relationships, but has also damaged intertribal relationships (very obvious in post-election clashes in Kenya), and even relationships within the tribes, because those who made their living working for the white settlers were often seen as traitors. During the Mau Mau struggle, which preceded independence from England, it is estimated that more than 100,000 Africans were killed in the war. The social cost to families and children is incalculable.

Rape was a weapon used to suppress the rebellion, and the psychological scars left by the struggles of the 1950s have never been dealt with in any way. By and large, the lot of women in rural Africa has not improved with national independence. Woman are conditioned to want less, expect less and receive less than men do, so they are underfed, underpaid and undereducated.

African countries have suffered from Western industrialisation, because the land has been taken from women (who originally made a living from it – they worked the land while the men looked after the herds) and used for cash crops – tea and coffee. Since it is increasingly difficult for them to earn a living, their social status has been undermined. Only men are head of households, with all the legal rights this involves. Sixty per cent of the illiterate people in the world are women; in some places it is as high as 85 per cent. Development plans often exclude any participation by women, and both the women and the nation suffer as a result.

Equality for women means having the same rights, responsibilities and opportunities as men, and that requires decision-making power. Too often the Maasai father is willing to sell his daughter into marriage to a man as old as himself. The mother, on the other hand, will do all in her power to prevent this. When a young girl has completed her primary education (if she is lucky enough to have a sponsor), she will do her best to get a place in secondary school, and even if it means being alienated from her father, she and her mother will try to get work of any kind to enable her to remain in school.

There is a practice among the Maasai women of working in groups to finance their needs. They meet in groups of about ten on a weekly basis. Each contributes about fifteen cents and a different woman is given the whole amount each week. This enables her to get her household utensils or other necessities. Elaine helps groups to aspire to little industries (for example, the making of beaded jewellery which is then sold at a profit). When the women come up with a good idea, they put a business plan together, and if Elaine thinks it is feasible then she will lend some of the money, but she is strict about having it repaid, so that others can have a chance.

In a better world we would have more nurturant power – power for the sake of others – enabling them to act independently for the good of all. It assumes the giftedness of others, and encourages that giftedness. Elaine Bannon, in her work with the people of Rombo, especially the women, is fostering that power and the mini co-ops are an important step in that direction. While Elaine's focus on clean water, education and health care will benefit all the people, it will help the women most. When one sees women with babies on their backs carrying containters of water on their heads and rolling other containers ahead with their feet for several kilometres, one realises how much the emancipation of women is linked to the availability of water! If you asked any African woman what would be the best gift she could receive, she would answer without hesitation, 'Water'.

Girls have made up the vast majority of children for whom Elaine has received school scholarships. That has to influence and enhance the position of future women of Rombo. She has taken seriously the words of Nelson Mandela: 'Freedom cannot be achieved unless the women have been emancipated from all forms of oppression.'

− 7 −
Education

IRELAND, A SMALL ISLAND on the edge of Europe, and far to the east of the vast American continent, suffered eight hundred years of foreign oppression and all its attendant disadvantages. The Famine of the mid-nineteenth century was somewhat similar to what Africa suffers every few years. The sad years of the 'hungry forties' decimated the population and caused an anger and bitterness that is slow to fade from the Irish psyche. Patriots such as the Young Irelanders, the Fenians, Irish Volunteers and the Citizen Army gave their lives in an armed struggle, while strategists like O'Connell, Parnell and Davitt tried the political route. After the huge upheaval of the Great War things began to shift, and though a bloody civil war took many of Ireland's best young men and created enormous rifts in our society, the infant nation held on for economic survival, and kept faith with its vision of a free and independent Ireland that would, in the words of the courageous patriot Robert Emmet, 'find its place among the nations of the world'.

Always conscious that a small country, with few natural resources, had to make the most of its brain power, and aware too of the huge advantage in having several indigenous religious congregations devoted to education, willing to place their personnel and resources at the service of the emerging nation, successive governments developed an educational system that stood Ireland in good stead as the twentieth century progressed. Up to 1969 there was free education for all at primary school level. After this children had access to free second-level education and, as the exchequer figures became healthier, free third-level education followed. In less than a century Ireland had moved from being a nation of downtrodden people, whose best chance for the future was emigration to England or America, into a country that was confident of its own ability to fashion its future and contribute to a new and prosperous Europe. The key to this enormous step forward was education.

Kenya today is not too unlike the Ireland of a century ago. It has suffered from foreign oppression and fought for independence. It has no valuable minerals or oilfields and, like the Ireland of the past, the majority of its people make their living on the land. However, the scourge of global warming, which has brought drought and floodings, has added another dimension to Kenya's struggle for economic independence. The population in the 1980s was 15 million; now, despite the ravages of AIDS and a life expectancy of only 49, it is 32 million. The unemployment level is at 40 per cent, while the GDP per head is $500 per annum (in Ireland it is €45,500 per annum). Add to this the lack of infrastructure, transport and reliable ways of communication, it becomes very difficult to set up a market economy, and disease in people, cattle and plant life in general makes for terrible frustration among a people who hold on to life by their fingertips.

Unlike Ireland, Kenya has not had a tradition of book learning. Even in the darkest days of our history there were hedge-school masters who travelled around Ireland and kept the fire of knowledge alive, at great cost to themselves. Going back to the early days of Christianity in Ireland, the monasteries were renowned places of learning, and the monks brought their treasures of knowledge and the ability to impart it to the European continent. The tribal learning in Kenya is mostly oral, and in a world that has almost gone beyond books and depends more and more on the computer, the learning available to the young Kenyan in his own tribe, though having many worthy values to hand on to a society moving at breakneck speed, unfortunately seems out of sync with the world of the third millennium. Globalisation is having its way and Kenya, if it is to survive, must advance in terms of education and technology.

Amazingly, the great leader of the Kenyan revolution, Jomo Kenyatta, was wise enough to insist that his country continue to have English as its second language (after Kiswahili). As a result, the schools founded by Irish missionaries in the capital, Nairobi, and the other major locations of population made it compulsory for subjects to be taught through English. This meant that bright pupils often got scholarships to universities in England and America, and were able to gain the highest qualifications. Nonetheless, the fact that children are sitting for examinations where they have to answer the questions, not in their tribal language, nor in the national language, but in a language that was spoken by the oppressor, makes the process of being educated difficult both at conscious and unconscious levels.

While the Maasai people were totally nomadic, schools were not seen as a priority. However, as drought and starvation have become endemic – thousands of cattle died of hunger in 2006 and a disease, known as Rift Valley Fever, decimated the herds in 2007 – people were forced to gravitate towards the cities in search of food. Here they swelled the ranks of the slum-dwellers and they soon realised that without some modicum of education there was no future for their children. They began to go to school. Gradually, word trickled back to the bush and a new sense of what was necessary for survival dawned.

As is the case in most countries, when governments are planning to build schools, the places furthest away from the large centres of population are the last to be considered, and the Kenyan government, struggling with the repayment of loans to the World Bank, was happy to turn a blind eye to the fact that many of its children would never get a chance to go to school. As a tribe, the Maasai, who roamed the huge Rift Valley, were very much in this category. Elaine saw the desperate need for education, and with her managerial ability to focus on the essentials she enlisted the help of foreign donors to provide for the building of schools. Up to this, most of the teaching was done outdoors, and when the rainy season came all classes had to be suspended. There were so few schools in the Rombo area that children often had to walk as many as fifteen kilometres each way to get basic education. When one child returning from school was killed by a hyena, the people appealed to Elaine to do something for them. The local people in Moilo gathered stones for the foundations and Elaine set about finding a generous donor. The Rotary Club, always to the fore in assisting her, were again extremely helpful, and family and friends were extraordinarily creative in their ways of raising funds.

The building of another school in the area was then undertaken at Lemongo. Here, Belgrove Senior Boys' School, Clontarf, and Electric Aid (part of ESB Ireland) provided money to build three classrooms, while AMREF (African Medical Research Foundation) paid for another two. That school is called Belgrove Primary School, Lemongo. The island of saints and scholars is functioning in a different way!

The funding required for building a school is only part of the story. The provision of desks, a blackboard and very basic cupboards for materials is almost as costly as the structure of the building, so another group of donors has to be found to meet these costs. In a country where wood is in short supply, and because the forests are precious for environmental reasons, furnishings are very expensive.

Regarding the system of remuneration for teachers, in the case of the two schools mentioned, the local people will pay an untrained teacher who has had second-level education until such time as the school is registered by the government. For this to happen the school will require proper toilet facilities, adequate seating and a sufficient number of pupils to justify the employment of a trained teacher and the payment of his or her salary.

In addition to the building of schools, wells as deep as ninety metres have to be dug so that the basic elements of hygiene will be available, and that children will be spared the terrible scourge of gastroenteritis, which can be fatal. Since each well costs about €2,500, plus the costs of plumbing, a lot of fund-raising is necessary before a school is ready to welcome the local children.

Elaine has set up a system of sponsorship so that children whose parents cannot possibly meet the school fees required will have a chance to be educated. When we talk about fees in Ireland we are talking about the cost of tuition, but fees in Kenya cover uniforms, books and often a meal during the day. Otherwise the children would be in rags and hungry – a poor way of giving them a sense of the value of the journey on which they are embarking. The hope is that these children will go on to higher education and then come back to be leaders in their tribe. Just as the American cheque played an important role in the education of Irish people in the past, so in the Kenya of today the hope is that those who have the ability will help their tribe and transform the Kenyan society of the future.

To take a possible and all too real example of how sponsorship could help a girl out of a life of servitude and poverty: Peninah (a popular name in Kenya) is nineteen years old. She belongs to a Maasai family, and her father is totally against educating the girls. Along with her sister, Charity, she has really struggled to stay in school. While still in primary school, both girls left home in the middle of the night and sought refuge at the local convent because their father had plans to have them circumcised and married off. Charity is currently in secretarial school as a result of sponsorship from Switzerland, but Peninah has been less fortunate. Their mother has been banished from the home for encouraging her daughters to seek education and their father recently destroyed the mud house where she and Peninah were living. A local teacher has given Peninah refuge and she is doing her very best to get any kind of work available to acquire fees for nursing school. The most she will earn in a day will be €1.70, and out of this she has to pay for food for herself and her mother. As the fee for nursing school is €1,200 per year, for three years, finding the fees is impossible unless there is sponsorship from abroad. When we realise that there is one health centre in the entire Rombo parish, a parish which covers an area of 562 square kilometres and has a population of more than 29,000, we can see how wonderful it would be to have an extra nurse!

Elaine has a wonderful sense of the importance of the now: when a young girl, Dorcas, who was in college in Tanzania, was sent home shortly before graduation because all her fees (of over €1,000) had not been paid, Elaine took off on a motorbike to the bank (thirty miles away) and Dorcas returned to finish her course.

One group of seven sisters is being educated by Elaine's receipt of sponsorship for them from Ireland. Their uncle was doing all in his power to get them to school. The sisters are from two different fathers, both of whom were brothers to the man who is now looking after them. He has four children of his own, and they are also being educated. He has a small farm and some animals, but has run up huge debts in his desire to do the best he can for the children. Such is his appreciation of education that he started a small nursery school in his own village. The teacher is a Maasai woman who goes without salary most of the time. Every time he meets Elaine he asks her to teach him some new words in English. Certainly the times are changing!

Third-level education is essential for the advancement of the whole Maasai tribe, but for most adults that is a very ambitious dream. One of the schools established through Elaine's campaigning has solar lamps and this enables those who never got a chance at education to at least attend classes in reading and writing at night. The adult education programme is also performing another enormously important social function. I have already mentioned that girls are circumcised and sold into marriage. Often, because this is a tribal custom, the men never think about its terrible effects on the women. In the adult education curriculum, talks are given separately to young men and women about the problems created by female genital mutilation. The men are shocked to learn that so much suffering results from this practice. An alternative rite of passage is being suggested, which would comprise of a celebration and talks on sexuality and health issues connected with reproduction.

Education has a long way to go as far as the Maasai people are concerned, but attitudes are changing and, as is so often the case in life, the crisis caused by a seemingly insurmountable obstacle gives rise to a whole new way of thinking and living. The fact that global warming has decreased the pasture lands for the cattle has meant that the young Maasai are looking to education with new hope and expectation.

– 8 –

Rotary International

I HAVE MENTIONED that Elaine had great support from her former associates in the corporate world. Not only did some, such as Matt Porter and his wife Mary Beth, support her with their personal encouragement, finance and expertise, they also opened the door to a wonderful source of help – Rotary International.

The first Rotary club was formed in Chicago, Illinois, USA in 1905 by Paul P. Harris. He was an attorney who wished to recapture in a professional club the same friendly spirit he had felt in the small town of his youth. The name 'Rotary' derived from the practice of rotating the early meetings among the members' offices. Rotary's popularity spread throughout the US in the decade that followed. By 1921 clubs had been formed in six continents. A year later the organisation adopted the name 'Rotary International'.

As Rotary grew, its mission expanded beyond serving the professional and social interests of its members.

Rotarians began pooling their resources and contributing their talents to help serve communities in need. Their dedication to this ideal is best expressed in their motto: 'Service above Self'. Rotary also embraced a code of ethics. During and after World War II rotarians became increasingly involved in promoting international understanding. With the establishment of the United Nations they played an active role in forwarding its ideals. They sponsor international and cultural exchanges, and in 1985 they made an historic commitment to immunise all of the world's children against polio. To date they have immunised more than one billion children against the dreaded disease. Their plans are continuously ambitious, as the needs in Third World countries become better known, and they are constantly expanding their efforts to address such pressing issues as environmental degradation, illiteracy, food scarcity and children at risk. The mission statement of Rotary International is to provide service to others, to promote high ethical standards and to advance world understanding, goodwill and peace through its fellowship of business, professional and community leaders. What a wonderful attitude to life, and what a vast and exciting programme for a world where acquisitiveness and selfishness leads to so much unhappiness on all sides!

Among Elaine's staunchest supporters has been a member of the Rotary Club in Ireland, Matt Porter. He has made trips to Rombo and has seen the needs for himself. He has played a very active part in raising funds for wells, water pipes, health centres and school buildings. The Rotary mission statement has been brought to life in his amazing and unceasing service of his fellow human beings.

In Elaine Bannon, the Rotary Club has found an ideal collaborator. The fact that she was awarded the prestigious Paul Harris award for her extraordinary contribution to building a better world shows how a vision formed more than a century ago is being fulfilled by a generous and courageous Dublin woman in the new millennium.

— 9 —
Destiny

A GROUP OF Mercy associates gathered around Elaine as she reflected on the past five years. She recalled that in her job as general manager and director of a successful company, she was able to go on as many as four foreign holidays a year. Kenya was a place that she had longed to visit. As a gift to herself for her fortieth birthday she went to this very beautiful country and fully enjoyed her stay. However, when she returned to work she became aware of how in her daily life she was under immense pressure from shareholders to make higher profits, and from those to whom she was selling, to give greater discounts. She began to notice that avarice was taking over in the world that she inhabited and she did not like it. In fact, as she put it, 'I began to feel sick of it all'.

Earlier in the book I outlined the steps through which she came to be in Rombo (where she now lives and works). As she thought about some of the formative events of the past five busy years, she zoned in on particular incidents that have stayed with her, and will stay with us. There was the awful reality of the little baby who was very badly burned when he fell into the open fire in the middle of the family's six-by-six-foot hut. The verdict of the health centre's nurse was: 'It took too long to get him here and infection has set in. I don't think he will make it.'

Then there was a twelve-year-old girl found sitting on Elaine's doorstep one morning at 6 a.m. in great distress because her father wanted to have her circumcised and sold into marriage in Tanzania – as he had done with her four sisters. Elaine had no money to get her into the safety of a boarding school, but she contacted the school at which the child was a good student to see what they could do. The next morning again at 6 a.m. she was there, only now her legs were torn from a beating at the hands of her father. This time Elaine took her into her own home (with the approval of the local chief) and kept her until she could find the money to get her into a boarding school where she would be safe.

A little boy of about thirteen stayed from early morning until early afternoon outside her office in the hope that the local chief might have business with Elaine, whereupon he would meet him and ask for a chance to go to school. Thankfully, he got this opportunity, because he lives near Lemongo where the school opened its doors in January 2008. He was part of the young crowd milling through the front door that first day!

What strikes me most about Elaine is her respect, love and admiration for the Maasai people. Often, with the best of intentions, people from the West who go to developing countries seem to unconsciously dismiss the values of those they have come to work with, and impose values that are foreign and often repugnant to the indigenous people. The life of Mahatma Gandhi shows another side to this. Gandhi went to England to pursue his studies in law. When he was qualified he went to practise his profession in South Africa. Apartheid was strong at the time, and when, as a professional, dressed according to Western custom, he tried to travel first class by train, he was unceremoniously ejected. Thus he began to rethink his position and subsequently embraced fully his Indian identity and all its ramifications. In later years he wore the simple dress of his native land, wove his own blanket and portrayed a quiet strength in leading his fellow countrymen in non-violent protests in the cause of freedom. Even when he travelled to the land of the oppressor (England), instead of seeming to aspire to be the equal of those with whom he negotiated, he wore his native dress and depended on the justice of his cause. He found, by experience, that integrity troubles the deceitful, gentleness confuses the arrogant, humility puzzles the aggressive, fair-mindedness disarms the prejudiced and non-violent steadfastness in face of injustice torments the bully. Now, a half-century after his death, his name is synonymous with dignity, courage and true leadership, and the story of his life is read in dozens of languages.

Some time ago, when speaking with an elderly missionary who had spent a lifetime in Kenya, I found that he was amazed that the Kenyans were able to manage their affairs so well when they won their freedom.

The unconscious arrogance, in even the most well-intentioned white people, often led them to believe that their way of doing things was the only way, and that when the reins of power were taken from the white minority and given to the indigenous people, there would be chaos! Unlike what happened in our own country, the change-over was without the horror of civil war. While (as is the case in any European country finding its own feet) there were teething problems, the native ability, especially in mastering different languages, and the pleasant personalities so characteristic of the Kenyans gave them great facility in negotiating the complex world of international politics. With ever-greater ease, they are establishing embassies in different countries – the latest of these in Ireland!

Ever-conscious of that old Irish saying, '*Beatha duine a thoil*' (a person finds life in doing the thing according to his own will), Elaine adopted a co-operative method of work. She is one of a group of four; the others – Elijah Kilempu, Joseph Nkanoni and Jonathon Kipanu – are Maasai men who understand their own people and have the advantage of knowing the subtleties of the language. In the various projects they have undertaken, the sponsorship from abroad has only been sought if the local people have done their share to deserve the input. For example, the trenches for the water pipes were dug by the women, the deep wells were the responsibility of the men and even the children gathered the stones needed for the foundations of the schools.

Elaine's destiny is interwoven with that of the Maasai people, and their destiny with hers. However, while faith and the guiding hand of God point the way, the natural gifts he has given to all must be employed in working out that destiny in the day-to-day struggles of life.

— 10 —

Elaine's Work — As Seen at First Hand

ON TUESDAY, 4 December 2007, through the kindness of Matt Porter, I set out, long before dawn, on a four-stage journey to Rombo. The first leg was to Amsterdam, where I changed planes for an eight-hour trip to Nairobi. There, Sr Liz Fletcher (the Provincial of the Mercy Sisters in Kenya) and Sr Maria NGui met me and brought me to one of the Mercy houses (Villa Maria) in Westlands. I was warmly welcomed, and though my stay was short (I had to be at the airport by 5.45 a.m.) I enjoyed meeting old friends and making new acquaintances. As I travelled through the city in the early morning, I remembered the Nairobi I had left twenty years before and I marvelled at the huge improvements. It was truly an international city — even in the early hours of the morning it was buzzing. However, I met with the same courtesy that I had remembered from airport officials and I was helped at every point with my luggage.

The trip to Mombasa was short, and when I arrived it was already very hot. Elaine and Elijah met me and we began the final lap of the journey. I was struck by the huge volume of traffic, mostly big trucks, and the road to Mombasa, which I had remembered as being narrow and badly maintained, was now a real highway where one could be tempted to go beyond the speed limit! Kenya is the gateway to East Africa and the signs of prosperity were obvious. Nonetheless, when we left the main road at Voi, things changed, and only that Elijah is an excellent driver, one could despair of making it to one's destination! The road goes through territory that is frequented by wild animals, elephants, gazelles and cheetahs, and we saw some as we passed. Last year Elaine was able to get a four-wheel drive (as a result of the combined charitable efforts of the Rotary Club and the people of north Dublin) but prior to this the car she used had broken down on this road, and Elijah stayed with it for a week until mechanics came from Mombasa to replace a broken axel. It had been a long and dangerous vigil, but he was given food and water by passing drivers, and he was eventually able to drive the car to the safety of home. If he had not stayed with it, it would be seen as fair game for anybody looking for a wheel or any other part!

Having travelled through all kinds of riverbeds and over rough roads, we finally reached our destination before dark. Elaine had arranged that I should sleep in the convent of the Sisters of St Francis (a native Kenyan congregation). I was delighted to meet the sisters there, who ran the local health centre and who worked very hard with almost no resources to provide the only health care available in the entire area of 562 square kilometres.

Day begins early in Africa, so I went to Mass at 7 a.m. The parish hall, where Mass was celebrated, was built by an Indian priest, Fr George Maylil. He had come to Rombo in the late 1980s, and though he hadn't the Maasai language and his knowledge of Kiswahili was poor, he managed to communicate through love. Using a panga (a type of machete), he had cut paths into the bush so that the women who needed the help of the health centre when they were giving birth, and those who were ill, or those who were coming to the sacraments would have a reasonably safe route. He built little churches at twenty-one outstations (all on hills), some as far as seventy kilometres away from his base, so that as often as possible these people could have his services. He also designed a church for Rombo, which, when completed, will be a place worthy of having the worship of God within its walls. (By the way, the Oblate Fathers in Inchicore, Dublin, donated very generously to help in the work, but things happen slowly in Africa!) Sadly, Fr George died suddenly in 2002. His family wanted to bring his body home for burial, but the Maasai are warriors, and they would not relinquish the remains of the one who meant so much to them! Now, six years later, they have a wonderful monument at his burial place and they talk about him as if he were still with them – and, of course, his spirit is with them still, and the spirit of his work and energies lives on because in 2002 (shortly after his death) Elaine decided to go and work with this loyal and beautiful community.

After Mass and breakfast with the sisters, I headed for Elaine's little house. I was met on the way by Joseph, one of the team that works with Elaine. Though it was only 8 a.m. he had come from his home (quite a distance away) and was watching out for me, lest I might go astray. Joseph was originally studying for the priesthood. He is very intelligent with a great faculty for language. He was with me almost all the time I was in Rombo and was a wonderful interpreter. Shortly before my arrival he had lost his twenty-four goats because they had eaten poisoned berries. Unfortunately, happenings of this kind are far from rare. However, when I commiserated with him, the response was, 'Life here is like that', and he quickly changed the subject to that of my journey!

The first thing I noticed was the fact that even at this early hour there were people queuing up outside Elaine's house with problems. There was Josephine, who had just finished in primary school and who, because she was bright, had been allocated a place in a secondary school. However, because they had no money, her father wanted to sell her into marriage. If she did not have the money that day for the school uniform in her new school then her place would be given to another. Thankfully, on a recent trip to Ireland Elaine had received sponsorship for her and the problem was solved. Other minor miracles followed and we then set out on a tour of the health centre. We were brought through the various treatment areas and the maternity ward by a wonderful Tanzanian nurse, Illuminata. If I were ill, she would be a person that I would like to have looking after me. She is a highly qualified nurse and midwife, and has done a course in counselling for people with AIDS. One of the problems she encounters is the reluctance of patients to take the retro-viral drugs, because, while the drugs stop the progression of the virus, they also cause depression, and for young mothers struggling to raise their children, this side effect complicates the issue severely. By the way, Illuminata is in her fifties; she works fourteen hours a day and earns €100 a month. With this monthly income, and with the help of a loan from Elaine, she has seen her son through Radiography in the University of Nairobi, and her daughter is in her first year at that university also. She was one of the most inspiring people I met during my time in Kenya.

As we left the clinic we learned that a woman had very recently died there of the AIDS virus. The body would not be released until the fees for her stay and the price of the petrol for the ambulance to bring her home were paid. Again, Elaine came to the rescue, and I became very aware that the small donations (as distinct from capital funding for schools, water pipes etc.) are extremely important: they help to provide the solution needed for crisis situations that may arise at any moment. I was reminded of the words of Catherine McAuley (foundress of the Sisters of Mercy): 'The poor want relief now; next week will be too late.' Shortly after this we met an elderly woman who was looking after her grandchildren – their mother had died of AIDS. One of the grandchildren had broken his arm three weeks before, but she had no money to bring him to the nearest hospital, which was thirty miles away. The Maasai people are independent, dignified people who will only ask for help in a real crisis. Again the availability of money due to small donations made it possible for Elaine to help.

Most of the remainder of the day was spent visiting women's groups. I was very moved by their welcome and their love and respect for Elaine. She has helped them to organise themselves to set up little businesses and in this way begin to be independent. Most of them have never been to school, but they have great practical ability and a love for their children which makes every sacrifice seem worthwhile. When I saw the inside of their huts and realised that there was no storage space of any kind, I quickly realised that storage space was unnecessary because they had nothing to store! These women danced and sang for us, and I came away with beautiful beaded jewellery that must have taken long hours of patient work to produce.

The last visit of that day was to the new school at Lemongo, of which I spoke earlier. Beside it, thanks to the Rotary Club, there is a water pump, and from this the school and the people in the surrounding area have clean water.

I mentioned earlier that there was only one health care centre for the whole area. Another is being built by the government, but, as often happens in these situations, the money has run out before the task has been completed. Each member of parliament is allocated money for his region and the local councillors exert pressure to make them spend the money on their particular projects. I noticed that for this clinic under construction a lot of money was spent on building a veranda in front to give shelter to patients while they are awaiting attention, but the result is that building on the actual treatment areas has been curtailed. There is a need for skilled people to supervise construction so that money will be used wisely. In the recent fraught elections, Joseph was elected as a councillor and I have great faith in his intelligence and common sense. The job of councillor carries no salary except about €100 per annum for expenses, so only people who have the good of the community at heart will be likely to seek election.

A woman called Irene impressed me enormously. She came from a political family and her father was one of those who, tired of the corruption of the Moi regime, staged an abortive coup and spent many years in prison as a result. When he was set free his health was so damaged that he died shortly afterwards. Irene is a teacher and a member of the church council. She is extremely bright and has great integrity. As I talked with her I was happy that Elaine had such good friends around her. The government may give a teacher to the new school at Lemongo and if this happens Irene would be willing to leave the school she is in (which is near her home) to give this new venture her best energies. Lemongo is a long way from her home and the terrain is difficult, but she is not a woman frightened of hardship.

Being a teacher, I found it easy to make friends with my African peers. Monica is in her early twenties, with dancing brown eyes full of mischief. She has sixty children in her class, but it does not seem to bother her. She was inspired by the life of Wangari Maathai (a Kenyan woman who won the Nobel peace prize in 2004). Her great hope would be to further her education by doing a MA over a period of four years at the University of

Nairobi. She intends to do this during her holiday periods. The only problem is that it would cost €1,000 per year. If I won the Lotto she would be high on my list! Thankfully we do not have to wait for the Lotto because an artist friend and his wife who is a lecturer in education is sponsoring Monica. Like Irene, Monica comes from a family where concern for real values was fostered. In a society where men found their identity in their herds, her father became a teacher, and he sought out young boys who had potential and took them from the fields into school. Often, when they were far from home he kept them in his own house. Many of the leaders in the present generation were his pupils.

Elaine's humble abode is an exciting place to be. It is a place where problems are discussed, but it is also a place where hopes and dreams are articulated. Such dreams are greeted with enthusiasm and the steps towards their realisation are planned. Books are discussed, passages read aloud and the great leaders of past and present are celebrated. The supply of coffee seems endless and the door is open to all.

Not all those with problems come to Elaine's door; some meet her on the road. When we were in Loitoktok we met a young woman who needed a lift home for herself and her sick child. She had walked a long journey in the morning and had left her baby (whom she was breastfeeding) with her mother. The child she had with her needed to be hospitalised, but she had to go home to nurse the baby. On the journey she explained that she had four children. She had been sold into marriage by her father, and she was the fourth wife of a man who constantly drank the equivalent of our poteen, and allowed his sons from three previous marriages to beat her up. She had returned to her mother. All of them lived in destitution and none of the children were in school. Joseph asked if she had been able to get the cattle that were her due. When she replied that she hadn't, he suggested that they go to the police and the local chief and get them. She begged that nothing be done, because she feared for her life. Elaine has subsequently helped this family with food and education on an ongoing basis.

One of the signs of poverty that reminded me of famine times in Ireland was the sight of people in the 'square' in the early hours of the morning hoping to get a day's work, so that they could earn money to buy food for their children. The sight of so many hungry children and animals is engraved in my memory and I feel it will continue to be one of my nightmares.

Another situation that will haunt me is that of a beautiful woman in her late thirties who suffers from AIDS. Mary Wambui had irrigation close to her home, and she and her husband had a good crop of maize. When she was diagnosed as being HIV positive, her husband suggested that they sell their crop and get treatment for her. The crop was sold, but he absconded with the money. She had a seventeen-year-old son who was working for a lorry driver. On one long journey the driver was carrying stolen goods, and they were followed by the police. The lad was unaware that there was any problem, and when the driver ran away the police shot the boy. Mary has a ten-year-old daughter who suffers from a heart condition. The tops of her fingers and toes are swollen and because of the difficulty she has with walking she misses a lot of school. However, she is very bright and her English is perfect. Elaine has arranged that she attend a school very near home for the coming year and is trying to get her to a specialist for a consultation. The third member of Mary's family, Leah, is a beautiful but sad-looking teenager. Again, thanks to Elaine, her education is being seen to and she is getting some counselling.

I could go on with numerous examples of how the power of one is being felt in southern Kenya, but I will just go quickly to the sad events that followed the recent elections. Rombo was not a place of violence, but the lack of food due to the drought made for enormous problems. The only way to get food was to buy from the nearest town, but the police had roadblocks everywhere. Eventually they were removed and Elaine's four wheel drive stood her in good stead when it came to transporting bags of maize and beans! Again St Joseph was busy. Elaine sent a text message to her mother saying that she needed €2,000 urgently so that she could mount a food programme. As luck, or St Joseph, would have it, between neighbours, friends and family, €2,000 had been lodged to the account the previous week! The power of one does not refer just to Elaine and people like her; it refers especially to the one who was the provider for the Holy Family!

Epilogue

As I come to the end of the book, I reflect on the genesis of this effort. Having known Elaine and her family for several years, I had always been impressed by their inclusiveness of people of all ages, races and religions. Whether it was the neighbour who needed to have her garden seen to, the child who had fallen and cut his knee, the Traveller woman who arrived without fail every Saturday or the French, Japanese or Romanian who came to Ireland in search of work or for language study, there was a warm inclusion of each in the Bannon family. When Elaine decided to work in Kenya, I was not surprised, but I did try to persuade her to join an established aid organisation. Having spent part of my life on the Kenyan mission, I knew what being in 'the bush' was like, and how wonderful it was to have the back-up of a religious community in Nairobi, to which I could go occasionally for respite or even a nice warm bath!

However, Elaine understood her own call and I now realise that being part of a big organisation can have its limitations too. Often, the established works have to be 'manned' at all costs, and the possibility of a wider vision sometimes is curtailed.

While thinking of ways to raise money, a friend suggested that it might be a good idea to have a gate collection in the parish in which I lived and in which Elaine had grown up. I approached my parish priest, Fr Brian McKay, and with characteristic generosity and enthusiasm he gave me every assistance. Emboldened by the success of that venture (it brought in €11,000), I asked another neighbouring parish priest, Fr Liam Murtagh, and he too was willing to give me the opportunity to speak to the people of Marino. Once more, we collected about the same amount. After one of the Masses here, Matt Porter came to me and suggested that I go and see Elaine's work on the ground, and that he would organise my ticket. This, together with the fact that many people had told me how the story of Elaine's bravery and generosity had inspired them, made me feel that I should write about her inspirational journey. I recalled that the life of Dr Tom Dooley, the US Catholic humanitarian who spent his working life helping the people of Vietnam, had given me huge incentive as a young person to work for something bigger than myself. I remembered too that during forty-five years in the classroom I could always get the pupils to come to life when I told them of how some 'ordinary' people like Sally Trench or Christina Noble transcended themselves and, with bravery and generosity, brought new hope to people in distress. So often I have witnessed Transition Year classes rise to the challenge of raising money for charities at home and abroad. Young people in Ireland today are just as idealistic as any who preceded them, when they believe in the cause.

During the summer of 2007 Ireland got more than its fair share of rain. One sunny morning as I was coming home from Mass, I met two young boys – Andrew and Austen. The former was born in South Africa and the latter in Ireland. They are half-brothers; Andrew, being the elder, was the spokesman. I suggested that to celebrate the arrival of the sun we should go to the nearest shop, where I would buy them ice-cream. They agreed with alacrity and we set out forthwith. When we arrived I asked them what they would like. Andrew promptly answered, 'Whatever you will give us will be very good'. The answer was so polite and so trusting that I was shocked. The owner of the shop, Alan, noticed that I was somewhat tongue-tied and so made a suggestion, to which Andrew answered, 'Thank you, sir, that will be lovely'. As the boys thanked me again, I suddenly realised that the fears I had about the book were there because I was focusing on my own limitations, and that if I had even a fraction of the trust these little boys had in me, a stranger, I would know that what the Father would send me in terms of inspiration on a day-to-day basis would be 'very good'. I no longer feared that perhaps my efforts would meet with ridicule, because there was Somebody else in the equation besides myself.

I have enjoyed recounting the journey of someone I admire greatly. I have been surprised and grateful for all the encouragement from family, friends and community. If even one person is inspired by reading about what I consider an extraordinary enterprise, then I will be delighted!

Afterword

SINCE MY VISIT to Kenya in December 2007, Elaine has been home for medical reasons. Thankfully, she returned with a clean bill of health and some extra money to forward her plans. A school where many of the children had no classrooms and were taught under a tree, without any means of writing or even a blackboard to show how writing might be done, will soon have two new classrooms. Another school will also get an extension, and the Dublin central branch of the Rotary Club is working hard to provide funds to get wells and water pipes for the town of Rombo. They have now found money to kit out a new health centre, and individuals have been sending donations to aid in the sinking of wells at strategic points, where villages can easily access it. This is enormous progress, and the health and well-being of the people at the southern end of the Rift Valley has been greatly enhanced. However, there is a very long road ahead. Only somebody as courageous as Elaine Bannon would continue to dream and to back up her dreams with the hard work that is required to make those dreams a reality.

Perhaps you would like to assist Elaine's work! The information below will enable you to see how best this can be done.

Nominally, there is universal education in Kenya, but the reality is that there are not enough schools, and the parents would not have the money required to provide for the payment of teachers. Until a school is well established, no salaries are paid. Often the journeys children have to walk necessitate their being given food at school so that they will have the energy to learn. Books and school equipment, including desks, are very expensive and must be provided without government aid. The fees vary according to the kind of school a child is attending. If he or she is too far from a school, then a boarding school is the only option, and obviously that will cost more than a day school. Roughy speaking, it costs €1 per day to keep a child in day primary or secondary school and €2–3 per day for third-level education. Cheques or direct debit for sponsoring children during their time in school can be forwarded to Joseph House of Hope, Bank of Ireland, Walkinstown, Dublin 12. The account number is 88233182. The sort code is 900287.

There is a separate bank account for people wishing to donate money to the development of wells and pipes, health centres etc.: Bank of Ireland, Killester, Dublin 3. The account name is Light of Maasai; account number 88490883; sort code 900594.

If at any time you would like an update on progress, please write to Sr Kathleen O'Keeffe, 14 Coolatree Close, Dublin 9, email kokrsm@hotmail.com, or phone 01 8377023. Thank you, and may you and those you love be blessed!